Rocky and Tony were painting.

Tessa was in the house.
Tessa had made a cake.

The cake was on the table.
Tessa went off to the shop to get some apples.

Rocky and Tony were happy with the painting.
They wanted Tessa to see it.
They left the paint and went into the house.

'Tessa, Tessa,' said Tony, 'look what we did!'
But Tessa was out.
'Tessa went out to get some apples,' said his mother.

Tessa bought the apples and went home.

'I have bought the apples,' said Tessa,
'but look at the cake!'
Tessa was cross. 'Who did it?'

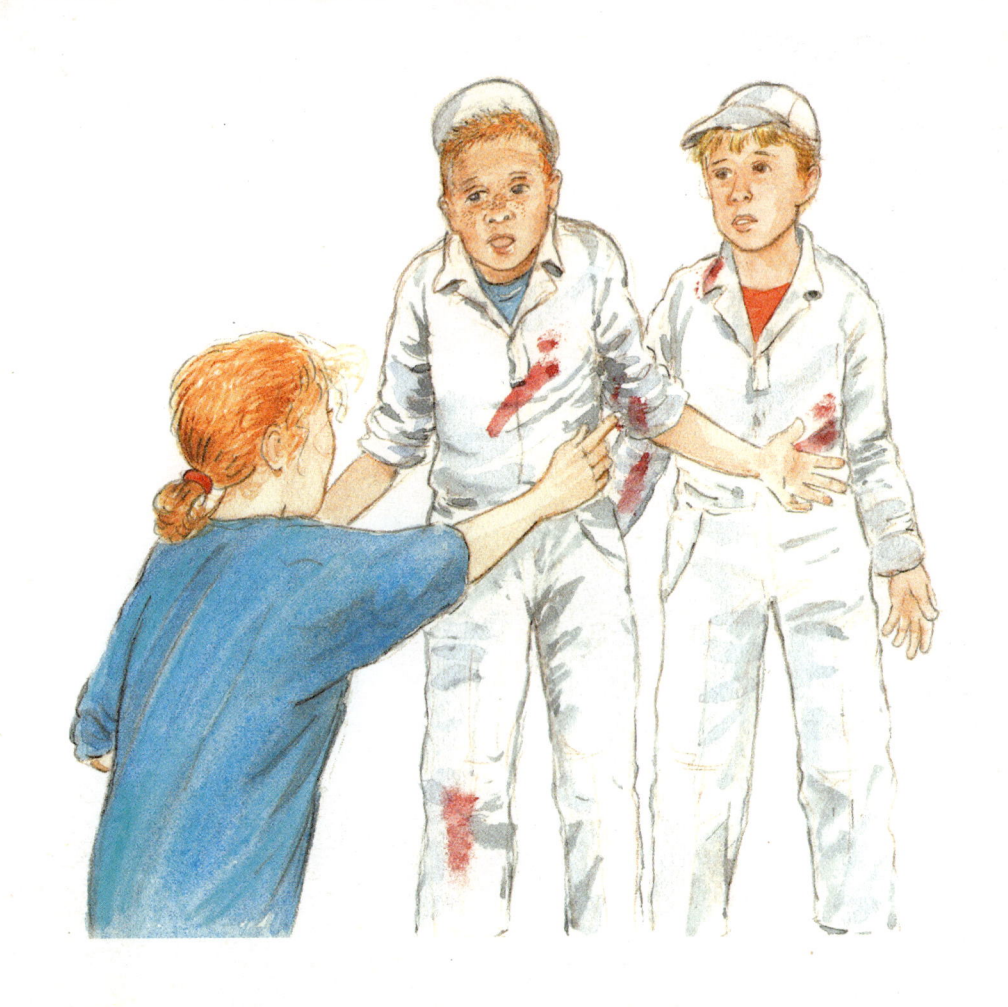

'Was it you, Rocky?' said Tessa.
'It was not,' said Rocky.
'Was it you, Tony?' said Tessa.
'No, it was not,' said Tony.

'Look at the table,' said Tessa, 'and look at the paint!'
'Look out of the window!' said Rocky.

They all ran out of the house and
followed the paint.

'It was my dog,' said Rocky.
'It was Max. He left paint on the cake!'

'Woof woof!'